THE AMERICAN REVOLUTION

History SparkNotes

Spark Educational Publishing
A Division of Barnes & Noble Publishing
120 Fifth Avenue
New York, NY 10011
www.sparknotes.com

ISBN 1-4114-0417-3

Please submit all comments and questions or report errors to *www.sparknotes.com/errors*.

Printed and bound in the United States

CONTENTS

Overview

Before and during the French and Indian War, from about 1650 to 1763, Britain essentially left its American colonies to run themselves in an age of salutary neglect. Given relative freedom to do as they pleased, the North American settlers turned to unique forms of government to match their developing new identity as Americans. They established representative legislatures and democratic town meetings. They also enjoyed such rights as local judiciaries and trials by jury in which defendants were assumed innocent until proven guilty. American shipping, although theoretically regulated by the Navigation Act, functioned apart from the mighty British fleet for more than a hundred years. Finally, the promise of an expansive, untamed continent gave all settlers a sense of freedom and the ability to start fresh in the New World.

After the French and Indian War, the age of salutary neglect was finished. Britain, wanting to replenish its drained treasury, placed a larger tax burden on America and tightened regulations in the colonies. Over the years, Americans were forbidden to circulate local printed currencies, ordered to house British troops, made to comply with restrictive shipping policies, and forced to pay unpopular taxes. Furthermore, many of those failing to comply with the new rules found themselves facing a British judge without jury. Americans were shocked and offended by what they regarded as violations of their liberties. Over time, this shock turned to indignation, which ultimately grew into desire for rebellion. In a mere twelve years—between the end of the French and Indian War in 1763 and the outbreak of the Revolutionary War in 1775—the colonists moved from offering nightly toasts to King George III's health to demonstrations of outright hostility toward the British Crown.

The American Revolution had profound consequences, not only for the American colonists but for the rest of the world as well. Never before had a body of colonists so boldly declared their monarch and government incapable of governing a free people. The Thomas Jefferson–penned Declaration of Independence was as unique as it was reasonable, presenting a strong, concise case for American rebellion against a tyrannical government. Since then, his declaration has been a model for many groups and peoples fighting their own uphill battles.

Summary of Events

The French and Indian War

The North American theater of the primarily European **Seven Years' War** was known as the **French and Indian War**. It was fought between Britain and France from 1754 to 1763 for colonial dominance in North America. British officials tried to rally public opinion for the war at the **Albany Congress** in 1754 but mustered only halfhearted support throughout the colonies. Nevertheless, American colonists dutifully fought alongside British soldiers, while the French allied themselves with several Native American tribes (hence the name "French and Indian War"). This war ended after the British captured most of France's major cities and forts in Canada and the Ohio Valley.

Pontiac's Rebellion

The powerful Ottawa chief **Pontiac**, who had no intention of allowing land-hungry whites to steal more tribal lands, united many of the tribes in the volatile Ohio Valley and led a series of raids on British forts and American settlements. British forces eventually squashed **Pontiac's Rebellion**. As a conciliatory gesture toward the Native Americans, Parliament issued the **Proclamation of 1763**, forbidding American colonists to settle on Native American territory unless native rights to the land had first been obtained by purchase or treaty.

The End of Salutary Neglect

The French and Indian War also motivated Parliament to end the age of **salutary neglect**. Prime Minister **George Grenville** began enforcing the ancient **Navigation Acts** in 1764, passed the **Sugar Act** to tax sugar, and passed the **Currency Act** to remove paper currencies (many from the French and Indian War period) from circulation. A year later, he passed the **Stamp Act**, which placed a tax on printed materials, and the **Quartering Act**, which required Americans to house and feed British troops.

Taxation Without Representation

The Sugar Act was the first fully enforced tax levied in America solely for the purpose of raising revenue. Americans throughout the thirteen colonies cried out against **"taxation without representation"** and made informal nonimportation agreements of certain British goods in protest. Several colonial leaders convened the **Stamp Act Congress** in New

York to petition Parliament and King George III to repeal the tax. In 1766, Parliament bowed to public pressure and repealed the Stamp Act. But it also quietly passed the **Declaratory Act**, which stipulated that Parliament reserved the right to tax the colonies anytime it chose.

THE TOWNSHEND ACTS AND BOSTON MASSACRE

In 1767, Parliament passed the **Townshend Acts**, which levied another series of taxes on lead, paints, and tea known as the **Townshend Duties**. In the same series of acts, Britain passed the **Suspension Act**, which suspended the New York assembly for not enforcing the Quartering Act. To prevent violent protests, Massachusetts Governor Thomas Hutchinson requested assistance from the British army, and in 1768, four thousand redcoats landed in the city to help maintain order. Nevertheless, on March 5, 1770, an angry mob clashed with several British troops. Five colonists died, and news of the **Boston Massacre** quickly spread throughout the colonies.

THE BOSTON TEA PARTY

In 1773, Parliament passed the **Tea Act**, granting the financially troubled **British East India Company** a trade monopoly on the tea exported to the American colonies. In many American cities, tea agents resigned or canceled orders, and merchants refused consignments in response to the unpopular act. Governor Hutchinson of Massachusetts, determined to uphold the law, ordered that three ships arriving in Boston harbor should be allowed to deposit their cargoes and that appropriate payments should be made for the goods. On the night of December 16, 1773, while the ships lingered in the harbor, sixty men boarded the ships, disguised as Native Americans, and dumped the entire shipment of tea into the harbor. That event is now famously known as the **Boston Tea Party**.

THE INTOLERABLE AND QUEBEC ACTS

In January 1774, Parliament passed the **Coercive Acts**, also known as the **Intolerable Acts**, which shut down Boston Harbor until the British East India Company had been fully reimbursed for the tea destroyed in the Boston Tea Party. Americans throughout the colonies sent food and supplies to Boston via land to prevent death from hunger and cold in the bitter New England winter. Parliament also passed the **Quebec Act** at the same time, which granted more rights to French Canadian Catholics and extended French Canadian territory south to the western borders of New York and Pennsylvania.

THE FIRST CONTINENTAL CONGRESS AND BOYCOTT

To protest the Intolerable Acts, prominent colonials gathered in Philadelphia at the **First Continental Congress** in autumn of 1774. They once again petitioned Parliament, King George III, and the British people to repeal the acts and restore friendly relations. For additional motivation, they also decided to institute a **boycott**, or ban, of all British goods in the colonies.

LEXINGTON, CONCORD, AND THE SECOND CONTINENTAL CONGRESS

On April 19, 1775, part of the British occupation force in Boston marched to the nearby town of **Concord**, Massachusetts, to seize a colonial militia arsenal. Militiamen of Lexington and Concord intercepted them and attacked. The first shot—the so-called "shot heard round the world" made famous by poet Ralph Waldo Emerson—was one of many that hounded the British and forced them to retreat to Boston. Thousands of militiamen from nearby colonies flocked to Boston to assist.

In the meantime, leaders convened the **Second Continental Congress** to discuss options. In one final attempt for peaceful reconciliation, the **Olive Branch Petition**, they professed their love and loyalty to King George III and begged him to address their grievances. The king rejected the petition and formally declared that the colonies were in a state of rebellion.

THE DECLARATION OF INDEPENDENCE

The Second Continental Congress chose **George Washington**, a southerner, to command the militiamen besieging Boston in the north. They also appropriated money for a small navy and for transforming the undisciplined militias into the professional **Continental Army**. Encouraged by a strong colonial campaign in which the British scored only narrow victories (such as at **Bunker Hill**), many colonists began to advocate total independence as opposed to having full rights within the British Empire. The next year, the congressmen voted on July 2, 1776, to declare their independence. **Thomas Jefferson**, a young lawyer from Virginia, drafted the **Declaration of Independence**. The United States was born.

Key People & Terms

People

John Adams
A prominent Boston lawyer who first became famous for defending the British soldiers accused of murdering five civilians in the **Boston Massacre**. Adams was a delegate from Massachusetts in the **Continental Congresses**, where he rejected proposals for reconciliation with Britain. He served as vice president to George Washington and was president of the United States from 1797 to 1801.

Samuel Adams
Second cousin to John Adams and a political activist. Adams was a failed Bostonian businessman who became an activist in the years leading up to the Revolutionary War. He organized the first **Committee of Correspondence** of Boston, which communicated with other similar organizations across the colonies, and was a delegate to both **Continental Congresses** in 1774 and 1775.

Joseph Brant
A Mohawk chief and influential leader of the **Iroquois** tribes. Brant was one of the many Native American leaders who advocated an alliance with Britain against the Americans in the Revolutionary War. He and other tribal leaders hoped an alliance with the British might provide protection from land-hungry American settlers.

Benjamin Franklin
A Philadelphia printer, inventor, and patriot. Franklin drew the famous "Join or Die" political cartoon for the **Albany Congress**. He was also a delegate for the **Second Continental Congress** and a member of the committee responsible for helping to draft the **Declaration of Independence** in 1776.

King George III
King of Great Britain during the American Revolution. George III inherited the throne at the age of twelve. He ruled Britain throughout the Seven Years' War, the French and Indian War, the American Revolution, the Napoleonic Wars, and the War of 1812. After the conclusion of the French and Indian War, his popularity declined in the

American colonies. In the **Declaration of Independence**, Thomas Jefferson vilifies George III and argues that his neglect and misuse of the American colonies justified their revolution.

GEORGE GRENVILLE
Prime minister of Parliament at the close of the French and Indian War. Grenville was responsible for enforcing the **Navigation Act** and for passing the **Sugar Act, Stamp Act, Currency Act**, and **Quartering Act** in the mid-1760s. He assumed, incorrectly, that colonists would be willing to bear a greater tax burden after Britain had invested so much in protecting them from the French and Native Americans.

PATRICK HENRY
A radical colonist famous for his "Give me liberty or give me death" speech. Henry openly advocated rebellion against the Crown in the years prior to the Revolutionary War.

THOMAS HUTCHINSON
Royal official and governor of **Massachusetts** during the turbulent years of the 1760s and early 1770s. Hutchinson forbade the British East India Company's tea ships from leaving Boston Harbor until they had unloaded their cargo, prompting disguised colonists to destroy the tea in the Boston Tea Party.

THOMAS JEFFERSON
Virginian planter and lawyer who eventually became president of the United States. Jefferson was invaluable to the revolutionary cause. In 1776, he drafted the **Declaration of Independence**, which justified American independence from Britain. Later, he served as the first secretary of state under President George Washington and as vice president to John Adams. Jefferson then was elected president himself in 1800 and 1804.

THOMAS PAINE
A radical philosopher who strongly supported republicanism and civic virtue. Paine's 1776 pamphlet *Common Sense* was a bestselling phenomenon in the American colonies and convinced thousands to rebel against the "royal brute," King George III. When subsequent radical writings of Paine's, which supported republicanism and condemned monarchy, were published in Britain, Paine was tried in absentia, found guilty of seditious libel, and declared an outlaw in England.

WILLIAM PITT, THE ELDER

British statesman who provided crucial leadership during the latter half of the French and Indian War. Pitt focused British war efforts so that Britain could defeat the French in Canada. Many have argued that without his leadership, Britain would have lost the war to the French and their allies.

PONTIAC

A prominent **Ottawa** chief. Pontiac, disillusioned by the French defeat in the French and Indian War, briefly united various tribes in the Ohio and Mississippi Valleys to raid colonists on the western frontiers of British North America between 1763 and 1766. He eventually was killed by another Native American after the British crushed his uprising. Hoping to forestall any future tribal insurrections, Parliament issued the **Proclamation of 1763** as a conciliatory gesture toward Native Americans and as an attempt to check the encroachment of white settlers onto native lands.

GEORGE WASHINGTON

A Virginia planter and militia officer who eventually became the first **president** of the United States. Washington participated in the first engagement of the French and Indian War in 1754 and later became commander in chief of the American forces during the **Revolutionary War**. In 1789, he became president of the United States. Although Washington actually lost most of the military battles he fought, his leadership skills were unparalleled and were integral to the creation of the United States.

TERMS

ALBANY CONGRESS

A congress convened by British officials in 1754 promoting a unification of British colonies in North America for security and defense against the French. Although the Albany Congress failed to foster any solid colonial unity, it did bring together many colonial leaders who would later play key roles in the years before the Revolutionary War. To support the congress, **Benjamin Franklin** drew his famous political cartoon of a fragmented snake labeled "Join or Die."

BATTLE OF LEXINGTON AND CONCORD

Two battles, fought on April 19, 1775, that opened the Revolutionary War. When British troops engaged a small group of colonial

militiamen in the small towns of **Lexington** and **Concord**, Massachu-setts, the militiamen fought back and eventually forced the British to retreat, harrying the redcoats on the route back to Boston using guerrilla tactics. The battle sent shockwaves throughout the colo-nies and the world, as it was astonishing that farmers were able to beat the British forces. This battle marked a significant turning point because open military conflict made reconciliation between Britain and the colonies all the more unlikely.

BATTLE OF SARATOGA
A 1777 British defeat that was a major turning point in the Revolu-tionary War. The defeat convinced the French to ally themselves with the United States and enter the war against Britain. Most histo-rians agree that without help from France, the United States could not have won the war.

BOSTON MASSACRE
An incident that occurred on March 5, 1770, when a mob of angry Bostonians began throwing rocks and sticks at the British troops who were occupying the city. The troops shot several members of the crowd, killing five. Patriots throughout the colonies dubbed the incident a "massacre" and used it to fuel anti-British sentiment.

BOSTON TEA PARTY
An incident that took place on December 16, 1773, when a band of Bostonians led by the **Sons of Liberty** disguised themselves as Native Americans and destroyed chests of tea aboard ships in the harbor. The Tea Party prompted the passage of the **Intolerable Acts** to punish Bostonians and make them pay for the destroyed tea.

FIRST CONTINENTAL CONGRESS
A meeting convened in late 1774 that brought together delegates from twelve of the thirteen colonies (Georgia abstained) in order to protest the **Intolerable Acts**. Colonial leaders stood united against these and other British acts and implored Parliament and King George III to repeal them. The Congress also created an association to organize and supervise a **boycott** on all British goods. Although the delegates did not request home rule or desire independence, they believed that the colonies should be given more power to legislate themselves.

FRENCH AND INDIAN WAR
A war—part of the **Seven Years' War** fought in the mid-1700s among the major European powers—waged in North America from 1754

to 1763. The British and American colonists fought in the war against the French and their Native American allies, hence the American name for the war. After the war, the British emerged as the dominant European power on the eastern half of the continent.

LOYALISTS

Those who chose to support Britain during the Revolutionary War. Loyalists were particularly numerous in the lower southern states, but they also had support from Anglican clergymen, wealthy citizens, and colonial officials. Thousands served in Loyalist militias or in the British army, while others fled to Canada, the West Indies, or England. A large majority of black slaves also chose to support Britain because they believed an American victory would only keep them enslaved. Native Americans sided with the British, too, fearing that American settlers would consume their lands if the United States won.

MERCANTILISM

An economic theory predominant in the 1700s that stipulated that nations should amass wealth in order to increase their power. Under mercantilism, the European powers sought new colonies in the Americas, Africa, and Asia because they wanted sources of cheap **natural resources** such as gold, cotton, timber, tobacco, sugarcane, and furs. They shipped these materials back to Europe and converted them into **manufactured goods**, which they resold to the colonists at high prices.

PATRIOTS

Those who supported the war against Britain. In January 1776, the English émigré philosopher and radical **Thomas Paine** published the pamphlet *Common Sense*, which beseeched Americans to rebel against the "royal brute," King George III, declare independence, and establish a new republican government. The pamphlet sold an estimated 100,000 copies in just a few months and convinced many Americans that the time had come to be free of Britain forever.

PONTIAC'S REBELLION

An uprising led by the Ottawa chief **Pontiac** against British settlers after the end of the French and Indian War. Pontiac united several Native American tribes in the Ohio Valley and attacked British and colonial settlements in the region. The forces under Pontiac laid siege to Detroit and succeeded in taking all but four of the fortified posts they attacked. Although the British army defeated Pontiac's

warriors and squelched the rebellion, Parliament issued the **Proclamation of 1763** as a conciliatory gesture to the Native Americans, recognizing their right to their territories.

Second Continental Congress

A meeting convened in 1775 by colonial leaders to discuss how to proceed after the recent **Battle of Lexington and Concord**. The Congress decided to try one last time to restore peaceful relations with Britain by signing the **Olive Branch Petition**. In the meantime, they prepared for national defense by creating a navy and the **Continental Army** and installing **George Washington** in command of the latter. At this point, many believed that war was inevitable.

Stamp Act Congress

A meeting convened in 1765 in New York to protest the **Stamp Act**. Delegates from nine colonies attended and signed petitions asking Parliament and King George III to repeal the tax. It was the first time colonial leaders united to protest an action by Parliament.

KEY PEOPLE & TERMS

Summary & Analysis

The French and Indian War: 1754–1763

Events

1754	George Washington's forces initiate French and Indian War Albany Congress convenes
1755	Braddock defeated
1758	British take Louisbourg
1759	British take Quebec
1760	British take Montreal
1763	Treaty of Paris ends French and Indian War Pontiac attacks Detroit British issue Proclamation of 1763

Key People

George Washington American general whose forces helped start the French and Indian War in western Pennsylvania in 1754

General Edward "Bulldog" Braddock British general who proved ineffective in fighting Native American forces during the French and Indian War

William Pitt Major British statesman during second half of the French and Indian War; successfully focused war efforts on defeating French forces in Canada

Pontiac Ottawa chief disillusioned by the French defeat in the war; organized unsuccessful uprising against settlers after the war's end

The Beginning of the War

Unlike the previous wars between European powers in the 1700s, the **French and Indian War** was begun in North America—in the heartland of the **Ohio Valley**, where both France and Britain held claims to land and trading rights. Westward-moving British colonists were particularly aggressive in their desire for new tracts of wilderness. The French, in order to prevent further British encroachment on what they believed to be French lands, began to construct a series of forts along the Ohio River. Eventually, the two sides came into conflict when a young lieutenant colonel from Virginia named **George Washington** attacked French troops with his small militia force and established Fort Necessity. Washington eventually surrendered after the French returned in greater numbers.

AMERICANS FIGHTING FOR THE BRITISH

The opportunity to serve side by side with British regulars during the war gave many Americans a sense of pride and confidence. It is estimated that some 20,000 Americans fought with the British against the French and Native American opposition. Washington, though he was defeated more than once during the war, was one of many colonists who gained valuable military and leadership skills that later proved useful during the Revolutionary War.

At the same time, though military service gave colonists a sense of pride, it also made many realize how different they were from the British regulars with whom they fought. Many British regulars disliked the colonists they were fighting to protect, and many British commanders refused to acknowledge the authority of high-ranking colonial militia officers.

COLONIAL DISUNITY

Furthermore, the British never managed to gain colonial support for the conflict. Many colonists, especially those living on the eastern seaboard far from the conflict, didn't particularly feel like fighting Britain's wars. Many colonial legislatures refused to support the war wholeheartedly until leading British statesman **William Pitt** offered to pay them for their expenses. Some colonial shippers were so disinterested in British policy that they actually shipped food to the French and its European allies during the conflict. In short, there was little colonial support for the war, but much colonial unity that was subversive to British war aims.

THE ALBANY CONGRESS

To bolster more colonial support for the French and Indian War, Britain called for an intercolonial congress to meet in Albany, New York, in 1754. To promote the **Albany Congress**, Philadelphia printer **Benjamin Franklin** created his now-famous political cartoon of a snake with the caption "Join or Die."

Despite Franklin's efforts, delegates from only seven of the thirteen colonies chose to attend. The delegates at the Albany conference agreed to support the war and also reaffirmed their military alliance with the Iroquois against the French and their Native American allies. But somewhat surprisingly, the delegates at Albany also sent Parliament recommendations for increased colonial unity and a degree of **home rule**. British ministers in London—as well as the delegates' own colonial legislatures—balked at the idea.

WAR SPREADS TO EUROPE

American colonists and the French waged undeclared warfare for two years until 1756, when London formally declared war against France. The conflict quickly spread to Europe and soon engulfed the Old World powers in another continental war (in Europe, the war was referred to as the **Seven Years' War**).

For Britain and France, this expansion of the war shifted the war's center from the Americas to Europe and thus transformed the struggle entirely. The fighting in North America became secondary, and both powers focused their attention and resources in Europe. However, despite the diversion of resources and manpower to Europe, many key battles in the war continued to be fought in the New World.

FRANCE'S STRONG START

During the initial years of the war, the French maintained the upper hand, as they repeatedly dominated British forces. The most notorious British defeat in North America came in 1755, when British **General Edward "Bulldog" Braddock** and his aide George Washington chose to attack the French **Fort Duquesne** in the Ohio Valley. After hacking through endless wilderness, their forces were slaughtered by the French and their Native American allies. This seemingly easy victory encouraged Native American tribes throughout the frontier to attack the British settlers encroaching on their lands.

BRITAIN'S RESURGENCE

After Britain officially declared war on France in 1756, British troops—many of whom were American colonists—invaded French Canada and also assaulted French posts in the West Indies. Not until the "Great Commoner" statesman William Pitt took charge of operations in London did Britain begin to turn the tide against France. Pitt focused the war effort on achieving three goals: the capture of the French Canadian cities **Louisbourg**, **Quebec**, and **Montreal**. He succeeded: Louisbourg fell in 1758, Quebec in 1759, and Montreal in 1760, giving the British a victory.

THE TREATY OF PARIS

The war ended formally with the **Treaty of Paris**, signed in 1763. Under the terms of the agreement, France was effectively driven out of Canada, leaving Britain the dominant North American power.

PONTIAC AND THE PROCLAMATION OF 1763

Despite the signing of the peace treaty, unofficial fighting between white settlers and Native Americans in the West continued for another three years. In one incident, a group of Native Americans, under the leadership of Ottawa chief **Pontiac** and supported by bitter French traders, killed roughly 2,000 British settlers, lay seige to Detroit, and captured most of the British forts on the western frontier. Though the British army quickly squelched **Pontiac's Rebellion**, Parliament, in order to appease Native Americans and to prevent further clashes, issued the **Proclamation of 1763**, which forbade British colonists from settling on Native American territory.

The Proclamation of 1763 angered Americans intensely: during the French and Indian War, they had believed they were fighting, at least in part, for their right to expand and settle west of the Appalachians. Many firmly believed that this land was theirs for the taking. The proclamation thus came as a shock. Many colonists chose to ignore the proclamation and move westward anyway. This issue was the first of many that would ultimately split America from Britain.

THE SUGAR AND STAMP ACTS: 1763–1766

EVENTS

1764	Britain begins to enforce the Navigation Act
	Parliament passes the Sugar and Currency Acts
1765	Parliament passes the Stamp and Quartering Acts
	Stamp Act Congress convenes in New York
1766	Parliament repeals the Stamp Act, passes the Declaratory Act

KEY PEOPLE

George III King of Great Britain throughout much of the colonial period; saw marked decline in popularity in the colonies after the French and Indian War

George Grenville Prime minister of Parliament; enforced the Navigation Act and passed the Sugar, Stamp, Currency, and Quartering Acts

Sons of Liberty Secretive groups of prominent citizens who led protests against British taxes and regulations; influence grew in 1765 after passage of the Stamp Act

GROWING DISCONTENTMENT WITH BRITAIN

During the period from 1763 to 1775, in the twelve years after the French and Indian War and before the outbreak of the Revolutionary War, colonial distrust of Britain grew markedly, and the emerging united national identity in America became more prominent. In just over a decade, proud British subjects in the American colonies became ardent anti-British patriots struggling for independence.

SALUTARY NEGLECT

Likewise, London's view of the colonies changed radically after the French and Indian War. Prior to the war, Parliament barely acknowledged the American colonists, treating them with a policy of **salutary neglect**. As long as the colonies exported cheap raw materials to Britain and imported finished goods from Britain (*see* Mercantilism, *below*), Britain was quite happy to leave them alone. After the war, though, the situation was radically different. By the end of the Seven Years' War, the British national debt had climbed over 100 million pounds, hundreds of thousands of which had been used to protect the British colonies in America.

MERCANTILISM

Britain's economy during the 1700s was based on **mercantilist** theories that taught that money was power: the more money a nation had in its reserves, the more powerful it was. Britain and other European powers, including France and Spain, actively sought new colonies in the Americas, Africa, and Asia to stimulate their economies and increase their wealth. Colonies provided cheap **natural resources** such as gold, cotton, timber, tobacco, sugarcane, and furs. These materials could be shipped back home to the mother country and converted into **manufactured goods**, which were resold to the colonists at high prices.

THE NAVIGATION ACTS

Immediately following the cessation of the French and Indian War, British Prime Minister **George Grenville** ordered the Royal Navy to begin enforcing the old **Navigation Acts**. Parliament had passed a major Navigation Act in 1651 to prevent other European powers (especially the Dutch) from encroaching on British colonial territories; the act required colonists to export certain key goods, such as tobacco, only to Britain. In addition, any European goods bound for the colonies had to be taxed in Britain. Although the law had existed for over one hundred years, it had never before been strictly enforced.

GRENVILLE AND THE SUGAR ACT

Because the French and Indian War had left Britain with an empty pocketbook, Parliament also desperately needed to restock the Treasury. Led by Grenville, Parliament levied heavier taxes on British subjects, especially the colonists. First, in 1764, Grenville's government passed the **Sugar Act**, which placed a tax on sugar imported from the West Indies. The Sugar Act represented a significant change in policy: whereas previous colonial taxes had been levied to support local British officials, the tax on sugar was enacted solely to refill Parliament's empty Treasury.

THE CURRENCY AND QUARTERING ACTS

The same year, Parliament also passed the **Currency Act**, which removed devalued paper currencies, many from the French and Indian War period, from circulation. In 1765, Parliament passed the **Quartering Act**, which required residents of some colonies to feed and house British soldiers serving in America. These acts outraged colonists, who believed the taxes and regulations were unfair. Many also questioned why the British army needed to remain in North America when the French and Pontiac had already been defeated.

THE STAMP ACT

Though the colonists disliked all of these acts, they particularly took offense to the 1765 **Stamp Act**. This tax required certain goods to bear an official stamp showing that the owner had paid his or her tax. Many of these items were paper goods, such as legal documents

SUMMARY & ANALYSIS

and licenses, newspapers, leaflets, and even playing cards. Furthermore, the act declared that those who failed to pay the tax would be punished by the vice-admiralty courts without a trial by jury.

Colonists were particularly incensed because the Stamp Act was passed in order to pay for the increased British troop presence in the colonies. Not only did the colonists feel that the troop presence was no longer necessary, they also feared that the troops were there to control them. This military presence, combined with the vice-admiralty courts and Quartering Act, made the Americans very suspicious of Grenville's intentions.

TAXATION WITHOUT REPRESENTATION

In protest, the American public began to cry out against **"taxation without representation."** In reality, most colonists weren't seriously calling for representation in Parliament; a few minor representatives in Parliament likely would have been too politically weak to accomplish anything substantive for the colonies. Rather, the slogan was symbolic and voiced the colonists' distaste for paying taxes they hadn't themselves legislated.

VIRTUAL REPRESENTATION

In defense, Grenville claimed that the colonists were subject to **"virtual representation."** He and his supporters argued that all members of Parliament—no matter where they were originally elected—virtually represented all British citizens in England, North America, or anywhere else. To the colonists, the idea of virtual representation was a joke.

THE STAMP ACT CONGRESS

Unwilling to accept the notion of virtual representation, colonists protested the new taxes—the Stamp Act in particular—using more direct methods. In 1765, delegates from nine colonies met in New York at the **Stamp Act Congress**, where they drafted a plea to King **George III** and Parliament to repeal the Stamp Act.

THE SONS AND DAUGHTERS OF LIBERTY

Other colonists took their protests to the streets. In Boston, a patriot group called the **Sons of Liberty** erected "liberty poles" to hang images of tax collectors and even tarred and feathered one minor royal official. People throughout the colonies also refused to import British goods. Homespun clothing became popular as colonial wives, or **Daughters of Liberty**, refused to purchase British cloth.

THE DECLARATORY ACT

Parliament eventually conceded and repealed the Stamp Act in 1766, which overjoyed the colonists. Quietly, however, Parliament also passed the **Declaratory Act** to reserve Britain's right to govern and "bind" the colonies whenever and however it deemed necessary.

The Declaratory Act proved far more damaging than the Stamp Act had ever been, because it emboldened Britain to feel that it could pass strict legislation freely, with few repercussions. It was during the aftermath of the Declaratory Act, from 1766 to 1773, that colonial resistance to the Crown intensified and became quite violent.

SUMMARY & ANALYSIS

The Boston Massacre and Tea Party: 1767–1774

Events

1767	Townshend Acts impose duties on goods, suspend the New York assembly
1768	British troops occupy Boston
1770	Parliament repeals all duties under the Townshend Acts except tax on tea Boston Massacre occurs
1773	Boston Tea Party occurs
1774	Parliament passes Coercive, or Intolerable, Acts Parliament passes Quebec Act

Key People

Thomas Hutchinson Governor of Massachusetts during early 1770s; instituted policies that prompted the Boston Tea Party

Charles Townshend British member of Parliament who crafted the 1767 Townshend Acts

The Townshend Acts

Parliament wasted little time invoking its right to "bind" the colonies under the **Declaratory Act**. The very next year, in 1767, it passed the **Townshend Acts**. Named after Parliamentarian **Charles Townshend**, these acts included small duties on all imported glass, paper, lead, paint, and, most significant, tea. Hundreds of thousands of colonists drank tea daily and were therefore outraged at Parliament's new tax.

Impact of the Townshend Acts

Fueled by their success in protesting the **Stamp Act**, colonists took to the streets again. **Nonimportation agreements** were strengthened, and many shippers, particularly in Boston, began to import smuggled tea. Although initial opposition to the Townshend Acts was less extreme than the initial reaction to the Stamp Act, it eventually became far greater. The nonimportation agreements, for example, proved to be far more effective this time at hurting British merchants. Within a few years' time, colonial resistance became more violent and destructive.

The Boston Massacre

To prevent serious disorder, Britain dispatched 4,000 troops to Boston in 1768—a rather extreme move, considering that Boston had only about 20,000 residents at the time. Indeed, the troop deployment quickly proved a mistake, as the soldiers' presence in the city only made the situation worse. Bostonians, required to house the soldiers in their own homes, resented their presence greatly.

Tensions mounted until March 5, 1770, when a protesting mob clashed violently with British regulars, resulting in the death of five Bostonians. Although most historians actually blame the rock-throwing mob for picking the fight, Americans throughout the colonies quickly dubbed the event the **Boston Massacre.** This incident, along with domestic pressures from British merchants suffering from colonial nonimportation agreements, convinced Parliament to repeal the Townshend Acts. The tax on tea, however, remained in place as a matter of principle. This decision led to more violent incidents.

THE TEA ACT
In 1773, Parliament passed the **Tea Act,** granting the financially troubled **British East India Company** an exclusive monopoly on tea exported to the American colonies. This act agitated colonists even further: although the new monopoly meant cheaper tea, many Americans believed that Britain was trying to dupe them into accepting the hated tax.

THE BOSTON TEA PARTY
In response to the unpopular act, tea agents in many American cities resigned or canceled orders, and merchants refused consignments. In Boston, however, Governor **Thomas Hutchinson** resolved to uphold the law and ordered that three ships arriving in Boston Harbor be allowed to despoit their cargoes and that appropriate payment be made for the goods. This policy prompted about sixty men, including some members of the **Sons of Liberty,** to board the ships on the night of December 16, 1773 (disguised as Native Americans) and dump the tea chests into the water. The event became known as the **Boston Tea Party.**

The dumping of the tea in the harbor was the most destructive act that the colonists had taken against Britain thus far. The previous rioting and looting of British officials' houses over the Stamp Act had been minor compared to the thousands of pounds in damages to the ships and tea. Governor Hutchinson, angered by the colonists' disregard for authority and disrespect for property, left for England. The "tea party" was a bold and daring step forward on the road to outright revolution.

THE INTOLERABLE ACTS
The Tea Party had mixed results: some Americans hailed the Bostonians as heroes, while others condemned them as radicals. Parliament, very displeased, passed the **Coercive Acts** in 1774 in a punitive effort to restore order. Colonists quickly renamed these acts the **Intolerable Acts.**

SUMMARY & ANALYSIS

Numbered among these Intolerable Acts was the **Boston Port Bill**, which closed Boston Harbor to all ships until Bostonians had repaid the British East India Company for damages. The acts also restricted public assemblies and suspended many civil liberties. Strict new provisions were also made for housing British troops in American homes, reviving the indignation created by the earlier **Quartering Act**, which had been allowed to expire in 1770. Public sympathy for Boston erupted throughout the colonies, and many neighboring towns sent food and supplies to the blockaded city.

THE QUEBEC ACT

At the same time the Coercive Acts were put into effect, Parliament also passed the **Quebec Act.** This act granted more freedoms to Canadian Catholics and extended Quebec's territorial claims to meet the western frontier of the American colonies.

THE REVOLUTION BEGINS: 1772–1775

EVENTS

1772	Samuel Adams creates first Committee of Correspondence
1774	First Continental Congress convenes in Philadelphia Boycott of British goods begins
1775	American forces win Battle of Lexington and Concord Second Continental Congress convenes in Philadelphia Second Continental Congress extends Olive Branch Petition King George III declares colonies in state of rebellion

KEY PEOPLE

John Adams Prominent Bostonian lawyer who opposed reconciliation with Britain during the Continental Congresses

Samuel Adams Second cousin to John Adams and ardent political activist

George III King of Great Britain; declared colonies in state of rebellion in 1775

Patrick Henry Fiery radical famous for his "Give me liberty or give me death" speech

George Washington Virginia planter and militia officer; took command of the Continental Army in 1775

COMMITTEES OF CORRESPONDENCE

In 1772, **Samuel Adams** of Boston created the first **Committee of Correspondence**, which was primarily an exchange of ideas in letters and pamphlets among members. Within a few years, this one committee led to dozens of similar discussion groups in towns throughout the colonies. Eventually, these isolated groups came together to facilitate the exchange of ideas and solidify opposition to the Crown. The Committees of Correspondence proved invaluable in uniting colonists, distributing information, and organizing colonial voices of opposition.

THE FIRST CONTINENTAL CONGRESS

In response to the **Intolerable Acts,** delegates from twelve of the thirteen colonies (Georgia chose not to attend) met at the **First Continental Congress** in Philadelphia in the autumn of 1774 to discuss a course of action. The delegates were all fairly prominent men in colonial political life but held different philosophical beliefs. **Samuel Adams, John Adams, Patrick Henry,** and **George Washington** were among the more famous men who attended.

Although rebellion against the Crown was at this point still far from certain, leaders believed grievances had to be redressed to Parliament and King **George III.** The delegates met for nearly two months and concluded with a written Declaration of Rights and requests to Parliament, George III, and the British people to repeal the **Coercive Acts** so that harmony could be restored.

SUMMARY & ANALYSIS

NATURAL RIGHTS

The First Continental Congress marked an important turning point in colonial relations with Britain. Although some delegates still hoped for reconciliation, the decisions they made laid the foundations for revolt. Even though American colonial leaders had petitioned Parliament and King George III to repeal taxes in the past, never had they boldly denounced them until this point, when they claimed that Britain's actions had violated their **natural rights** and the principles of the English constitution.

This appeal to natural rights above the king or God was groundbreaking because it justified and even legalized colonial opposition to the Crown. It converted the riotous street mobs into people justly defending their freedoms. In other words, the Americans were not in the wrong for resisting British policy. Rather, Britain was to blame because it had attempted to strip Americans of their natural rights as human beings. Thomas Jefferson later extrapolated these legal appeals in the Declaration of Independence.

THE BOYCOTT

The Continental Congress delegates decided that until the Coercive Acts were repealed, a stronger system of **nonimportation agreements**, including a new **boycott** of all British goods, should be organized and administered throughout the colonies. Patriotic colonists argued that the purchase of any British-produced goods—especially those goods made from American raw materials—only perpetuated the servile relationship the colonies had to London under the system of **mercantilism**.

COMMITTEES OF OBSERVATION AND SAFETY

The Congress therefore created the **Committees of Observation and Safety** and gave them the task of making sure no citizens purchased British merchandise under the authority of the Continental Association. The Congress also attempted to define the exact relationship Britain had with America and the degree to which Parliament could legislate. Although the Congress did not request home rule, it did claim that colonial legislatures should be entrusted with more responsibilities.

The Committees of Observation and Safety had a profound effect on American colonial life. As British officials shut down or threatened to shut down town legislatures and councils throughout the colonies, the committees often became de facto governments. Many established their own court systems, raised militias, legislated against Loyalist demonstrations, and eventually coordinated efforts with other observation committees in nearby communities. Also, most of these committees were democratically elected by community members and were thus recognized by patriotic colonists as legitimate supervisory bodies. Their creation and coordination helped spread revolutionary ideas and fervor to the countryside and later smoothed the transition to democracy after independence.

THE BATTLE OF LEXINGTON AND CONCORD

By 1775, colonial resentment toward Britain had become a desire for rebellion. Many cities and towns organized volunteer militias of **"minutemen"**—named for their alleged ability to prepare for combat at the drop of a hat—who began to drill openly in public common areas.

On April 19, 1775, a British commander dispatched troops to seize an arsenal of colonial militia weapons stored in **Concord**, Massachusetts. Militiamen from nearby **Lexington** intercepted them and opened fire. Eight Americans died as the British sliced through them and moved on to Concord.

The British arrived in Concord only to be ambushed by the Concord militia. The "shot heard round the world"—or the first shot of many that defeated the British troops at Concord—sent a ripple throughout the colonies, Europe, and the rest of the world. The British retreated to Boston after more than 270 in their unit were killed, compared to fewer than 100 Americans. The conflict became known as the **Battle of Lexington and Concord**.

The minutemen's victory encouraged patriots to redouble their efforts and at the same time convinced King George III to commit military forces to crushing the rebellion. Almost immediately, thousands of colonial militiamen set up camp around Boston, laying siege to the British position. The battle initiated a chain of events, starting with the militia siege of Boston and the Second Continental Congress, that kicked the Revolutionary War into high gear.

THE SECOND CONTINENTAL CONGRESS

The **Second Continental Congress** was convened a few weeks after the Battle of Lexington and Concord to decide just how to handle the situation. Delegates from all thirteen colonies gathered once again in Philadelphia and discussed options. The desire to avoid a war was still strong, and in July 1775, delegate **John Dickinson** from Pennsylvania penned the **Olive Branch Petition** to send to Britain. All the delegates signed the petition, which professed loyalty to King George III and beseeched him to call off the troops in Boston so that peace between the colonies and Britain could be restored. George III eventually rejected the petition.

WASHINGTON AND THE CONTINENTAL ARMY

Despite their issuance of the Olive Branch Petition, the delegates nevertheless believed that the colonies should be put in a state of defense against any future possible British actions. Therefore, they set aside funds to organize an army and a small navy. After much debate, they also selected **George Washington** to command the militia surrounding Boston, renaming it the **Continental Army**. Washington was a highly respected Virginian plantation owner, and his leadership would further unite the northern and southern colonies in the Revolution.

THE BATTLE OF BUNKER HILL

The delegates' hopes for acknowledgment and reconciliation failed in June 1775, when the **Battle of Bunker Hill** was fought outside Boston. Although the British ultimately emerged victorious, they suffered over 1,000 casualties, prompting British officials to take the colonial unrest far more seriously than they had previously. The engagement led King George III to declare officially that the colonies were in a state of rebellion. Any hope of reconciliation and a return to the pre-1763 status quo had vanished.

AMERICAN SOCIETY IN REVOLT: 1776–1777

EVENTS

1776	Thomas Paine writes *Common Sense*
1777	Vermont adopts a state constitution prohibiting slavery Iroquois begin to raid colonial settlements in western New York and Pennsylvania

KEY PEOPLE

George Washington Commander of the Continental Army

Nathanael Greene Aide to Washington; one of the highest-ranking and most respected American generals in the war

Baron von Steuben German commander who helped George Washington and Nathanael Greene train the Continental army

Thomas Paine Radical philosopher who strongly supported republicanism; wrote 1776 pamphlet *Common Sense*, which was a best-seller in the American colonies

Joseph Brant Mohawk chief who advocated alliance with Britain against American forces in the Revolutionary War

TRAINING THE CONTINENTAL ARMY

As the colonies prepared themselves for war, new militias were formed throughout America, primarily to defend local communities from British aggression. Other units, however, rushed to join their comrades in Boston as soon as every man had a musket. Under the strict command of **George Washington**, **Nathanael Greene**, and the German **Baron von Steuben**, this ragtag collection of undisciplined militiamen eventually became the well-trained **Continental Army**.

POPULAR SUPPORT FOR THE WAR

When the Revolutionary War began, Britain made a costly and ultimately fatal error in assuming that opposition to British policies came only from a core group of rabble-rousing ringleaders such as Washington, Jefferson, and the Adams cousins. The British believed, incorrectly, that if they arrested these men, the revolt would collapse and the minutemen would return to their homes. They failed to understand that a significant majority of Americans disliked British rule and desired something better. Historians estimate that the majority of eligible American men served at some point in the Continental Army, the militias, or both.

PATRIOTIC WOMEN

Many American women supported the war effort as well. Some particularly daring women chose to serve as nurses, attendants, cooks, and even spies on the battlefields. Others, such as the famous **"Molly

SUMMARY & ANALYSIS

Pitcher" (a woman named Mary Hays McCauly, who fought in her husband's place) and **Deborah Sampson** (who disguised herself as a man) saw action in battle. Most women, however, fought the war at home. As more and more husbands and fathers left home to fight, more and more wives and mothers took to managing the farms and businesses. A majority of women helped by making yarn and home-spun necessities such as socks and underwear, both to send to militiamen and to support the boycott of British goods.

COMMON SENSE

The radical English author and philosopher **Thomas Paine** helped turn American public opinion against Britain and solidify the emerging colonial unity with his January 1776 pamphlet *Common Sense*, which denounced King George III as a tyrannical "brute." Paine, reasoning that it was unnatural for the smaller England to dominate the larger collection of American states, called on Americans to unite and overthrow British rule so that they could usher in an era of freedom for humanity. Inspiring and easy to read, *Common Sense* stirred the hearts of thousands of Americans and persuaded many would-be Loyalists and fence-sitters to fight for independence. The pamphlet caused a huge sensation throughout the colonies and sold over 100,000 copies within a few months of its first printing.

THE LOYALISTS

Although most Americans supported the decision to break away from Britain and declare independence, about one-third of the colonists did not. These **Loyalists** were heavily concentrated in the lower southern colonies but could also be found in concentrated pockets throughout other regions, including the North.

The Loyalists had several reasons for choosing to support Britain. Some, including many wealthy merchants, Anglican clergymen, and officials, disagreed with Parliament's policies but felt that it was not right to challenge British rule. Others were political conservatives who preferred the status quo. Many ethnic minorities, including blacks and Native Americans, also backed Britain, fearful that victorious white Americans would trample their rights.

One hundred thousand Loyalists fled to Canada, England, and the West Indies before and during the war. Those who stayed faced persecution, especially in the northern colonies. In the lower southern colonies, however, many pro-British colonial men formed Loyalist militias. Tens of thousands of Loyalists also joined the British army to fight for king and country.

NATIVE AMERICANS

Native Americans were particularly fearful of future American expansion into their lands, and the majority of tribes chose to support Britain. In particular, the influential Mohawk chief **Joseph Brant** worked tirelessly to convince the Iroquois tribes to support the British. As a result of his efforts and those of others like him, thousands of Iroquois, Creek, Cherokee, Choctaw, and other warriors joined forces with the British and coordinated independent raids on American arsenals and settlements along the western frontier.

The Native American decision to ally themselves with the British and raid American outposts and towns proved in the end to be a fatal one. Most believed that the British were a sure bet and that the rebellious colonies stood almost no chance of winning. The ultimate British surrender was a huge loss for Native Americans: white settlers were already pushing westward, and after the war, they felt justified in their taking of native lands.

AFRICAN AMERICANS

Blacks, too, generally supported the British because an American victory would only keep them in bondage. Although roughly 5,000 blacks did serve in militias for the United States, most who had the opportunity chose to flee to British and Loyalist areas that promised freedom from slavery. Consequently, colonies both north and south lost tens of thousands of slaves.

To some degree, blacks fared better after the war than before. Faced with the somewhat embarrassing predicament of supporting the premise that "all men are created equal," as stated in the Declaration of Independence, while at the same time practicing human bondage, many states, such as Vermont, eventually abolished slavery. Other states legislated more gradual forms of emancipation. As a result, the number of free blacks in the United States skyrocketed into the tens of thousands by the end of the century. Slavery was by no means a dead institution (as the early 1800s proved), but these liberal decisions made during the war were significant steps forward on the road to equality.

UNDECIDED COLONISTS

Finally, some men and women were neither patriots nor Loyalists and opted to take a wait-and-see approach. Civilian casualties remained low throughout the war, so such fence-sitting was an attractive alternative for some colonists. Some of the colonies, however, tried to curb the number of free riders by passing laws that essentially ordered citizens to choose sides. Able-bodied men who failed to join militias were prosecuted in some colonies for failing to show support for the patriotic cause.

THE DECLARATION OF INDEPENDENCE: 1776

EVENTS

June 7	Second Continental Congress begins to debate independence
July 2	Second Continental Congress votes to declare independence
July 4	Delegates sign Declaration of Independence

KEY PEOPLE

Thomas Jefferson Virginia statesman who drafted the Declaration of Independence
John Adams Massachusetts delegate at the Continental Congress; assisted Jefferson with revisions to the Declaration of Independence
Benjamin Franklin Pennsylvania delegate at the Continental Congress; assisted Jefferson with revisions to the Declaration of Independence
George III King of Great Britain throughout the American Revolution

VIRGINIA PROPOSES INDEPENDENCE

At a meeting of the Second Continental Congress in the summer of 1776, **Richard Henry Lee**, a delegate from Virginia, proposed that the American colonies should declare their independence from Britain. Delegates debated this proposal heavily for a few weeks, and many returned to their home states to discuss the idea in state conventions.

By this point—after the Battle of Lexington and Concord, the Battle of Bunker Hill, and George III's rejection of the Olive Branch Petition—the thought of independence appealed to a majority of colonists. By July 2, 1776, the Continental Congress, with the support of twelve states (New York did not vote), decided to **declare independence**.

JEFFERSON AND THE DECLARATION OF INDEPENDENCE

Congress then selected a few of its most gifted delegates, including **Benjamin Franklin**, **John Adams**, and **Thomas Jefferson**, to draft a written proclamation of independence. Jefferson was chosen to be the committee's scribe and principal author, so the resulting **Declaration of Independence** was a product primarily of his efforts.

Jefferson kept the Declaration relatively short and to the point: he wanted its meaning to be direct, clear, and forceful. In the brief document, he managed to express clearly the ideals of the American cause, level weighty accusations against George III, offer arguments to give the colonies' actions international legitimacy, and encapsulate the American spirit of freedom and unity. In his first draft, Jefferson also wrote against slavery, signifying that people were fundamentally equal regardless of race as well—but this portion was stricken from the final document. Nevertheless, Jefferson's words gave hope to blacks as well as landless whites, laborers, and women, then and for generations to come.

LIFE, LIBERTY, AND THE PURSUIT OF HAPPINESS

The Declaration's second paragraph begins the body of the text with the famous line, "We hold these truths to be self-evident, that all men are created equal, that they are endowed by their Creator with certain unalienable Rights, that among these are Life, Liberty, and the pursuit of Happiness." With these protections, any American, regardless of class, religion, gender, and eventually race, could always strive—and even sometimes succeed—at improving himself via wealth, education, or labor. With those seven final words, Jefferson succinctly codified the American Dream.

THE SOCIAL CONTRACT

Jefferson argued that governments derived their power from the people—a line of reasoning that sprang from the writings of contemporary philosophers including **Jean-Jacques Rousseau** and **Thomas Paine**. Both had argued that people enter into a **social contract** with the body that governs them and that when the government violates that contract, the people have the right to establish a new government. These notions of a contract and accountability were radical for their time, because most Europeans believed that their monarchs' power was granted by God. The Declaration of Independence thus established a new precedent for holding monarchies accountable for their actions.

ABUSES BY GEORGE III

In the Declaration, Jefferson also detailed the tyrannical "abuses and usurpations" that George III committed against the American colonies. Jefferson claimed that the king had wrongly shut down representative colonial legislatures, refused to allow the colonies to legislate themselves, and convened legislatures at inconvenient locations. He also accused the king of illegally assuming judicial powers and manipulating judges and the court system. Finally, Jefferson claimed that George III had conspired with others (other nations and Native Americans) against the colonists, restricted trade, imposed unjust taxes, forced American sailors to work on British ships, and taken military actions against Americans. Jefferson noted that the colonists had repeatedly petitioned the king to try to restore friendly relations but that he had consistently ignored them. Americans had also appealed to the British people for help on several occasions, again to no avail.

Jefferson concluded that, in light of these facts, the colonists had no choice but to declare independence from Britain and establish a new government to protect their rights. He stated that in order to achieve this goal, the independent states would come together to become the **United States of America**.

SIGNING OF THE DECLARATION

Jefferson's bold document was revised in the drafting committee and then presented to the Congress on July 4, 1776. The Congress's members felt that Jefferson's case was strong enough that it would convince other nations that America was justified in its rebellion. The thirteen states unanimously approved of the Declaration of Independence, and the United States was born.

SUMMARY & ANALYSIS

THE REVOLUTIONARY WAR: 1775–1783

EVENTS

1775	Battle of Lexington and Concord
	Second Continental Congress convenes
1776	Jefferson writes Declaration of Independence
1777	Battle of Saratoga
1778	France and United States form Franco-American Alliance
1779	Spain enters war against Britain
1781	British forces under Cornwallis surrender to Washington at Yorktown
1783	Peace of Paris signed to end war

KEY PEOPLE

George Washington Commander of the Continental army
Lord Charles Cornwallis Commander of British forces that surrendered at Yorktown

BRITISH STRENGTHS

When war erupted in 1775, it seemed clear that Britain would win. It had a large, well-organized land army, and the **Royal Navy** was unmatched on the sea. Many of the British troops in the Revolutionary War were veterans who had fought in the French and Indian War. On the other hand, the Americans had only a collection of undisciplined militiamen who had never fought before. The American navy was small and no match for the thousand ships in the royal fleet. The state of the army did improve after **George Washington** whipped the **Continental Army** into a professional fighting force, but the odds still seemed heavily stacked in Britain's favor.

AMERICAN STRENGTHS

Nonetheless, the Americans believed that they did have a strong chance of success. They had a lot at stake: unlike the British, they were fighting on their home turf to protect their own homes and families. Perhaps most important, they were also fighting a popular war—a majority of the colonists were patriots who strongly supported the fight for independence. Finally, though most Americans had no previous military experience, their militia units were usually close-knit bands of men, often neighbors, who served together in defense of their own homes. They elected their own officers—usually men who did have some military training but who also knew the territory well. This native officer corps was a great source of strength, and as a result, American morale was generally higher than morale in the Royal Army.

Geography in the War

Geography also gave the Americans an advantage that proved to be a major factor in the war's outcome. To the British forces, the North American terrain was unusually rugged: New England was rocky and cold in winter, the South was boggy and humid in the summer, and the western frontier was almost impenetrable because of muddy roads and thick forests. In addition, because American settlements were spread out across a vast range of territory, the British had difficulty mounting a concentrated fight and transporting men and supplies. American troops, on the other hand, were used to the terrain and had little trouble. Finally, the distance between England and the United States put a great strain on Britain, which spent a great deal of time, energy, and money ferrying soldiers and munitions back and forth across the Atlantic.

The Battle of Saratoga

After numerous battles, the turning point in the war came in 1777 at the **Battle of Saratoga** in upstate New York. When American forces won, their victory encouraged **France** to pledge its support for the United States in the **Franco-American Alliance** of 1778. A year later, **Spain** followed suit and also entered the war against Britain. Spain, hoping to see Britain driven out of North America, had tacitly supported the Americans by providing them with munitions and supplies since the beginning of the war. Their entry as combatants took pressure off the Americans, as Britain was forced to divert troops to fight the Spanish elsewhere. Finally, **the Netherlands** entered the war against Britain in 1780.

Continuing Popular Support

Though the war went on for several years, American popular support for it, especially after France and Spain entered the fray, remained high. The motivation for rebellion remained strong at all levels of society, not merely among American military and political leaders. Many historians believe that it was this lasting popular support that ultimately enabled the United States to fight as long as it did. Although the United States did not really "win" the war—there were no clearly decisive battles either way—it was able to survive long enough against the British to come to an impasse. French and Spanish assistance certainly helped the Americans, but without the grassroots support of average Americans, the rebellion would have quickly collapsed.

SUMMARY & ANALYSIS

Whigs in England Against the War

Meanwhile, support in England for the war was low. In Parliament, many **Whigs** (a group of British politicians representing the interests of religious dissenters, industrialists, and others who sought reform) denounced the war as unjust. Eight years of their carping, combined with the Royal Army's inability to win a decisive victory, fatigued the British cause and helped bring the Revolutionary War to an end.

The Surrender at Yorktown

Fortified by the Franco-American Alliance, the Americans maintained an impasse with the British until 1781, when the Americans laid siege to a large encampment of British forces under **Lord Charles Cornwallis** at **Yorktown**, Virginia. Scattered battles persisted until 1783, but the British, weary of the stalemate, decided to negotiate peace.

The Peace of Paris

The war came to an official close in September 1783, when Britain, the United States, France, and Spain negotiated the **Peace of Paris**. The treaty granted vast tracts of western lands to the Americans and recognized the United States as a new and independent country. The last British forces departed New York in November 1783, leaving the American government in full control of the new nation.

STUDY QUESTIONS & ESSAY TOPICS

Always use specific historical examples to support your arguments.

STUDY QUESTIONS

1. *"Americans were still professing their loyalty to George III and their desire for peaceful reconciliation as late as 1775. Had Britain accepted the Second Continental Congress's Olive Branch Petition, the Revolutionary War could have been avoided." Support or refute this claim using historical evidence.*

Even though delegates at the Second Continental Congress sent the Olive Branch Petition to George III requesting reconciliation, the recent skirmishes and hostile American public opinion made peaceful resolution unlikely, if not impossible. The delegates of the Continental Congress appeared aware of this inevitability themselves, for at the same time that they wrote their final petition to George III, they also made defensive provisions for a navy and an army, the latter to be commanded by George Washington. Moreover, even if the delegates truly believed that peaceful reconciliation was possible, it is doubtful the American public shared this belief. The Committees of Correspondence had by 1775 become powerful distributors of anti-British propaganda to both city dwellers and rural settlers alike.

In addition, the organization and rallying that enabled the boycott on all British goods turned many colonists into patriotic Americans. This desire for independence was confirmed at the Battle of Lexington and Concord and the Battle of Bunker Hill, in which simple farmers refused to retreat from the powerful British army and instead stood their ground. Thus, even though Continental Congress delegates were still petitioning for peace as late as 1775, it is highly unlikely that peace was truly possible.

2. *What did American colonists mean by "No taxation without representation"?*

American colonists rallied behind the popular cry "No taxation without representation" to protest the taxes and other legislation forced upon them by a Parliament that contained no American representatives. Colonial Americans valued their own representative legislatures and believed it unfair that they had to subject themselves to a legislative body thousands of miles away. British Prime Minister George Grenville, however, justified the lack of American representatives in Parliament by citing the theory of "virtual representation," which stipulated that Parliamentarians, no matter where originally elected, acted in the interests of all British subjects in the world.

Despite the American colonists' desire for representation, though, "No taxation without representation" was more a symbolic protest than anything else. In reality, colonial American representatives in Parliament would have been too few in number and would have had too little political power to make much difference. Instead, the colonists' rallying cry was based on principle, a simple articulation that they wanted more freedom and power to govern their own colonial legislatures, and less interference from Parliament.

3. *Which had a more profound impact on American anti-British sentiment, the 1765 Stamp Act or the 1766 Declaratory Act? Use specific examples from history to support your argument.*

Although colonists protested the 1765 passage of the Stamp Act vehemently and even violently, the barely noticed Declaratory Act of 1766 had a much more profound effect on American-British relations in the long run. When Parliament repealed the Stamp Act in 1766 after protests in the colonies, it quietly passed the Declaratory Act, which reaffirmed Britain's right to pass legislation regarding the American colonies anytime it chose. This legislative carte blanche plagued Americans from that point on until war erupted in 1775.

In 1767, Parliament used the Declaratory Act to justify the Townshend Acts, which levied taxes on tea and other items. The tax prompted angry objections, some as extreme as the Boston Tea Party, in which a group of colonists destroyed thousands of dollars' worth of British tea by dumping it in Boston Harbor. Parliament also cited the Declaratory Act in 1774 to justify the Coercive Acts, or Intolerable Acts, which shut down Boston Harbor and required Bostonians to pay damages for the tea they had destroyed. Both the Townshend Acts and the Intolerable Acts—backed by the Declaratory Act—brought Americans closer to outright rebellion than the Stamp Act ever had.

SUGGESTED ESSAY TOPICS

1. *Analyze the reasons for escalating anti-British sentiment in the American colonies during the prewar decade from 1765 to 1775.*

2. *Was the First or the Second Continental Congress more significant in the years leading up to the Revolutionary War?*

3. *What were nonimportation agreements and the boycott? Which had a greater effect on American-British relations?*

4. *Explain how three of the following altered Americans' perceptions of Britain during the years 1763 to 1775. Which affected colonists the most and why?*

   a) the French and Indian War
   b) virtual representation
   c) Samuel Adams
   d) the Declaratory Act
   e) the boycott of British goods
   f) Thomas Paine

5. *Compare and contrast Thomas Jefferson's Declaration of Independence with Thomas Paine's pamphlet "Common Sense." Which had the greater effect on revolutionary America? Use specific examples to support your argument.*

REVIEW & RESOURCES

QUIZ

1. What was the Seven Years' War called in the American colonies?

    A. King Philip's War
    B. Pontiac's Rebellion
    C. The War of 1812
    D. The French and Indian War

2. All of the following are true about the French and Indian War *except*

    A. Most Native Americans, fearing encroaching white settlers, sided with the British
    B. The war was the result of long-standing border disputes in the Ohio Valley
    C. Great Britain emerged as the dominant colonial power in North America
    D. It was begun by George Washington

3. What did Parliament's Proclamation of 1763 do?

    A. Forbade those living in newly acquired French Canada to settle south of the Great Lakes
    B. Granted the American colonists free settlement rights in the Ohio Valley
    C. Forbade American colonists to settle west of the Appalachian Mountains
    D. Created a Stamp Tax on all legal documents, licenses, and paper goods

4. Benjamin Franklin's famous "Join or Die" political cartoon was drawn

    A. In 1754 to support the Albany Congress
    B. In 1765 to support the Stamp Act Congress
    C. In 1774 to support the First Continental Congress
    D. In 1775 to support the Second Continental Congress

5. Which piece of legislation was *not* a consequence of the French and Indian War?

   A. The Proclamation of 1763
   B. The Coercive Acts
   C. The Sugar Act
   D. The Stamp Act

6. Why did Pontiac lead a Native American uprising against British and American colonists?

   A. He felt betrayed after he had supported them in the French and Indian War
   B. He was angry at the increasing loss of Native American lands to colonial settlers
   C. He was working with the French who sought to retake Quebec
   D. He was trying to create a pan-Indian nation of tribes united against all Europeans

7. After the French and Indian War, British Prime Minister George Grenville believed all of the following *except*

   A. Britain was justified in raising colonial taxes
   B. Britain should exert a greater degree of control over its American colonies
   C. Parliament should restrict the issue of currency in the colonies
   D. Britain should grant the colonies home rule

8. Why did Americans hate the Sugar Act and the Stamp Act?

   A. They were the first revenue taxes Parliament had ever levied on the colonists
   B. Those who failed to pay the new taxes would by tried by vice-admiralty courts
   C. They were based on the theory of virtual representation
   D. All of the above

9. "Virtual representation" was the idea that

   A. All members of Parliament, no matter where they came from, represented all British subjects throughout the world equally
   B. Slaves' interests were represented by their masters in colonial legislatures
   C. Thomas Jefferson was speaking for all oppressed people in the British Empire when he wrote the Declaration of Independence
   D. The physical world is just a representation of the spiritual world

10. All of the following were consequences of the Stamp Act *except*

   A. Americans protested and even rioted in cities and towns throughout the colonies
   B. Tax collectors were hanged in effigy and tarred and feathered
   C. Delegates met at the Stamp Act Congress to prepare for war
   D. Americans stopped importing certain goods from Britain

11. What did mercantilist economic theory stipulate?

   A. That nations should lower tariffs and promote free trade so that all might benefit
   B. That nations should establish colonies to provide cheap natural resources and closed markets for finished goods
   C. That nations should seek to establish monopolies on key resources in order to gain power over other countries
   D. That nations should promote free enterprise and protect public property in order to become more powerful

12. What were nonimportation agreements?

    A.   Mandatory bans on all British imports
    B.   Mandatory bans on some British imports
    C.   Voluntary bans on all British goods
    D.   Voluntary bans on some British goods

13. When Parliament repealed the Stamp Act in 1766, it simultaneously passed

    A.   The Declaratory Act
    B.   The Currency Act
    C.   The Quartering Act
    D.   The Townshend Acts

14. Why did Prime Minister Grenville began enforcing the Navigation Acts?

    A.   To punish Bostonians after the Boston Tea Party
    B.   To delegitimize the small navy created by the Second Continental Congress
    C.   To tighten British control over American imports and exports
    D.   To protect American shipping from the French navy during the French and Indian War

15. The Coercive, or Intolerable, Acts were passed in response to

    A.   The Boston Tea Party
    B.   The Stamp Act riots
    C.   The Boston Massacre
    D.   The Battle of Lexington and Concord

16. British troops were sent to occupy Boston in 1768 after

    A.   Bostonians threatened to assassinate the royal governor
    B.   The Boston Tea Party
    C.   Bostonians vehemently protested the Townshend Acts
    D.   Riots broke out in New York and Philadelphia

17. The Boston Tea Party took place after

    A. The governor of Massachusetts refused to allow tea
       ships to leave the harbor before unloading their cargoes
    B. The Dutch East India Company refused to ship tea to
       the American colonies
    C. British officials increased the price of tea by passing the
       Townshend Acts
    D. The Continental Association boycotted tea

18. Why did American colonists hate the Quebec Act?

    A. It permitted Canadians to settle on New England lands
    B. It extended Quebec lands and granted more rights to
       French Catholics
    C. It took shipping contracts from Bostonian shippers and
       granted them to Quebecois shipping companies
    D. All of the above

19. Why did royal officials disband the New York colonial
    legislature in 1767?

    A. Legislators were preparing to proclaim their
       independence from Great Britain
    B. Legislators were dispatching militiamen to protect key
       arsenals near the harbor
    C. Legislators failed to enforce the Quartering Act
    D. All of the above

20. Even though Parliament repealed almost all of the
    Townshend Acts, it retained the tax on tea because

    A. The tea tax produced a lot of revenue
    B. The revenue earned from the tax paid for the British
       troops occupying Boston
    C. Parliament wanted Americans to know it always
       maintained the right to tax the colonies
    D. Americans were willing to pay the tea tax in exchange
       for eliminating the other taxes

21. What effect did the passage of the Coercive, or Intolerable, Acts have?

    A. They encouraged colonial leaders to convene the First Continental Congress
    B. They intensified anti-British sentiment throughout the colonies
    C. They prompted many Americans to send food and winter supplies to Boston
    D. All of the above

22. What did delegates at the First Continental Congress do?

    A. Petitioned King George III and Parliament to repeal the Intolerable Acts
    B. Declared the American colonies in a state of rebellion against Great Britain
    C. Asked Parliament for home rule
    D. Declared the Intolerable Acts null and void

23. When it first convened in 1775, the Second Continental Congress did all of the following *except*

    A. Sign the Olive Branch Petition
    B. Declare war on Great Britain
    C. Create a national army and navy
    D. Designate George Washington commander-in-chief of the Continental Army

24. The "shot heard round the world" refers to

    A. The first shot fired by victorious farmers at Lexington and Concord against British troops
    B. Aaron Burr's lethal bullet that killed Alexander Hamilton in duel
    C. The gunshot that assassinated John F. Kennedy
    D. Babe Ruth's "called shot" at Wrigley Field on October 1, 1932

REVIEW & RESOURCES

25. Committees of Observation and Safety were significant in the
     years just before the Revolutionary War for all of the
     following reasons *except*

     A.   They became the de facto town governments
     B.   They enforced the boycott on British goods
     C.   They raised town militias
     D.   They printed paper money

26. What were the Committees of Correspondence?

     A.   A Loyalist attempt to foster pro-British sentiment
          throughout the colonies
     B.   Secret societies that tried to foment war
     C.   Groups of people throughout the colonies who
          exchanged letters and essays containing pro-republican
          ideas
     D.   The groups of men who organized the Boston Massacre
          and Tea Party

27. Thomas Paine's 1776 pamphlet *Common Sense*

     A.   United the colonists against Britain
     B.   Claimed it was unnatural for a small country to
          dominate a large one
     C.   Encouraged Americans to rebel immediately and create
          a republican government
     D.   All of the above

28. What did Joseph Brant do during the Revolutionary War?

     A.   United many Native American tribes against the United
          States
     B.   United many Native American tribes against Britain
     C.   Convinced many Native American tribes to remain
          neutral
     D.   Tried in vain to unite Native American tribes under a
          common leader

29. During the Revolutionary War, black slaves

    A. Mostly supported the United States
    B. Mostly supported Britain
    C. Were divided over whom they should support
    D. Did not care who won

30. American Loyalists drew support from all of the following groups *except*

    A. New Englanders
    B. The colonies of the lower South
    C. Clergymen
    D. Wealthy merchants

31. What did British commanders assume, erroneously, at the beginning of the Revolutionary War?

    A. That most American colonists wanted to rebel against Britain
    B. That the desire to rebel was felt only by a few select ringleaders
    C. That most black slaves would be willing to fight for their freedom
    D. That the Canadians would help them fight the Americans

32. Which of the following documents set forth the belief that "all men are created equal, that they are endowed by their Creator with certain unalienable Rights, that among these are Life, Liberty, and the pursuit of Happiness"?

    A. The Constitution
    B. The Bill of Rights
    C. The Declaration of Independence
    D. The Articles of Confederation

REVIEW & RESOURCES

33. In the Declaration of Independence, Thomas Jefferson wrote
    that King George III had committed all of the following
    crimes against the American people *except*

    A.   Illegally assuming judicial powers
    B.   Disbanding representative legislatures
    C.   Levying unfair taxes
    D.   Interfering with negotiations for the Louisiana
         Purchase

34. In the Declaration, Jefferson argued that government should
    only be overthrown when it

    A.   Fails repeatedly to act in the interests of its people
    B.   Uses military force against its own people
    C.   When it levies unfair taxes on the people
    D.   All of the above

35. Jefferson wrote in the Declaration that the American people
    had petitioned Britain to redress grievances on several
    occasions. The colonists petitioned to redress grievances on
    all of the following occasions *except*

    A.   The Stamp Act Congress
    B.   The Albany Congress
    C.   The First Continental Congress
    D.   The Second Continental Congress

36. The Declaration of Independence accomplished all of the
    following *except*

    A.   Enumerated abuses by King George III
    B.   Justified American rebellion
    C.   United all the colonies together in a common struggle
         against Britain
    D.   Brought France into the war on the side of the
         Americans

37. Jefferson argued in the Declaration that governments derive their power from

    A. God
    B. Parliament
    C. The people
    D. The military

38. The term "salutary neglect" refers to

    A. Congress's consideration for blacks serving in the Continental Army
    B. Britain's treatment of French Canadians until the passage of the Quebec Act
    C. Britain's treatment of the American colonies prior to the French and Indian War
    D. Male attitudes toward women and the right to vote prior to 1776

39. Why was the 1777 Battle of Saratoga a turning point in the Revolutionary War?

    A. It forced Britain to recognize its former colonies as an independent nation
    B. It was the first American victory and boosted morale in the Continental Army
    C. It convinced the French to ally themselves with the United States against Britain
    D. It convinced British commanders that the war was futile and a waste of time

40. With which country did the United States forge a military alliance in 1778?

    A. Spain
    B. France
    C. Russia
    D. Austria

41. All of the following gave Americans an advantage over the
     British in the Revolutionary War *except*

     A.   Geography
     B.   Popular support for the war
     C.   Their offensive strategy
     D.   Parliament's deeply divided opinions on the war

42. Why did geography play a significant role in the
     Revolutionary War?

     A.   Britain was forced to fight a long war thousands of
          miles away from home
     B.   America had no center that Britain could strike to end
          the war quickly
     C.   Americans had experience fighting on the difficult
          terrain
     D.   All of the above

43. Which of the following was one of the Americans' greatest
     strengths in the Revolutionary War?

     A.   The native officer corps
     B.   The highly disciplined militias
     C.   The experienced Continental Army
     D.   The powerful merchant marine

44. What did the Peace of Paris do?

     A.   Ended the French and Indian War
     B.   Ended the Revolutionary War
     C.   Ended the War of 1812
     D.   Ended Shays's Rebellion

45. The Olive Branch Petition was drafted by delegates at the

     A.   Albany Congress
     B.   Stamp Act Congress
     C.   First Continental Congress
     D.   Second Continental Congress

46. What was Britain's greatest advantage over the United States in the Revolutionary War?

   A.   Its powerful army and navy
   B.   The widespread support for war among the British people
   C.   The army's experience with military operations in North America
   D.   All of the above

47. Britain's lack of enforcement of the Navigation Acts from 1650 until 1763 is an example of

   A.   Virtual representation
   B.   Mercantilism
   C.   Salutary neglect
   D.   An "abuse and usurpation" listed in the Declaration of Independence

48. From whom did Americans receive tacit support at the beginning of the Revolutionary War?

   A.   Russia
   B.   French Canada
   C.   Irish rebels also fighting British rule
   D.   Spain

49. The Proclamation of 1763 was issued primarily in response to

   A.   French protests that Americans from the British colonies were encroaching on their territory
   B.   Native American attacks on white American settlers along the western frontier
   C.   Appeals made by the Albany Congress
   D.   Protests that American cities were becoming too crowded

50. How did many patriotic American women support the Revolutionary War?

    A.   Making yarn and homespun goods to send to troops and to uphold the boycott

    B.   Serving as nurses, attendants, and combatants on the battlefields

    C.   Assuming traditional male roles on farms and in business

    D.   All of the above

ANSWER KEY

1. D; 2. A; 3. C; 4. A; 5. B; 6. B; 7. D; 8. B; 9. A; 10. C; 11. B; 12. D; 13. A;
14. C; 15. A; 16. C; 17. A; 18. B; 19. C; 20. C; 21. D; 22. A; 23. B; 24. A;
25. D; 26. C; 27. D; 28. A; 29. B; 30. A; 31. A; 32. C; 33. C; 34. A; 35. B;
36. D; 37. C; 38. C; 39. C; 40. B; 41. C; 42. D; 43. A; 44. B; 45. D; 46. A;
47. C; 48. D; 49. B; 50. D

Suggestions for Further Reading

BAILYN, BERNARD. *Ideological Origins of the American Revolution*. Cambridge: Harvard University Press, 1992.

COUNTRYMAN, EDWARD. *The American Revolution*. New York: Farrar, Straus and Giroux, 2003.

HIBBERT, CHRISTOPHER. *Redcoats and Rebels: The American Revolution Through British Eyes*. New York: W.W. Norton, 2002.

LECKIE, ROBERT. *George Washington's War: The Saga of the American Revolution*. New York: HarperCollins, 1993.

LIELL, SCOTT. *46 Pages: Thomas Paine, Common Sense, and the Turning Point to Independence*. Philadelphia: Running Press, 2003.

MAIER, PAULINE. *American Scripture: Making the Declaration of Independence*. New York: Random House, 1998.

MORGAN, EDMUND S. *The Birth of the Republic: 1763–89*. Chicago: University of Chicago Press, 1993.

RAPHAEL, RAY. *A People's History of the American Revolution: How Common People Shaped the Fight for Independence*. New York: HarperCollins, 2002.

VAN TYNE, CLAUDE H. *The Loyalists in the American Revolution*. Rochester, New York: Simon Publications, 2002.

WOOD, GORDON S. *The American Revolution: A History*. New York: Random House, 2002.

REVIEW & RESOURCES

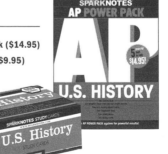